Signature Dishes & Original Recipes
from The Magic Ovens of

The Kitchen Witch Catering Cookbook

Mary Miller Thrasher

Copyright ©2007 Mary Miller Thrasher
Publication Date: January 2008

Maximilian Press Colophon is a registered trademark of
Maximilian Press Publishers

Book designed by Mary Thrasher
Graphic Design by M. Middleton
Editing by Maximilian

Manufactured in the United States of America

09 08 07 06 05 04 03 02 01
ISBN:978-1-930211-88-9

The paper used in this publication meets the minimum requirements of
ANSI/NISO Z39.48-1992 (R1997)

Published and Printed by:
Maximilian Press Publishers
920 So. Battlefield Blvd.
Suite 100, Chesapeake, VA 23322
757-482-2273

Acknowledgements

Tammy Lee Thrasher, Lindalyn Dentel, Chip and Pamela Fraser, Bill, Blanche and Dolly, Pamela Lucas, Sara Metzer, Kathleen Mulligan, Margaret Miller Doyle Hibbs Miller, Tammy Cross, Suzette Caldera, Jo Ruth Patterson, Kathy Ritchie Frierson, Billy and Beverly, Rusty, Trey and all of my family, friends, and customers who pushed me on... it's finally done!

Thank you.

Forward

Do I know the Kitchen Witch? You bet! I have been enjoying her food and creativity for about 50 years. I have watched her develop as a chef and proudly observed her talents for quite some time. Her imagination amazes me, her gift for concoction staggers me, and her recipes border on the magical.

But then again, one can expect me to be somewhat partial. After all, the Kitchen Witch is my sister!

Now, having admitted my bias, let me explain some of our history so you can appreciate what I appreciate. We were blessed to have a couple of grandmothers, mother, father, and aunts who enjoyed food and it's preparation. Learning "secrets" of how to and why you should, only added to Mary's aka the Kitchen Witch, ability to put things together the way they should be. Whether it was a sauce, a dessert, breads, grilling, sautéing, baking, broiling, or frying meats and seafood, or any number of dishes featuring fresh vegetables and fruit, Mary took what she needed from her family and friends, chefs and cooks that she worked with, and the New Restaurant School in NYC...and then she improvised and improved!

No one that I know has more artistic ability than Mary. She is an artist, not only in the kitchen, but also with paints, fabrics, room décor (for the cosmopolitan feng shui). In short, she is the polar opposite of boring!

Thus, when you put an artist in the kitchen, you can expect the food to look good, and it does. But more important, it tastes great. Mary's flair makes you want to eat and enjoy each mouthful because of its rich taste and perfect texture.

Having been an owner of restaurants, I think I have a pretty good idea of what is exceptional.

And I can certainly attest to Mary's focus on her product. She is organized which is a rarity for those who are creative. Her dishes emanate quality and once more (because you can't say it enough), the tastes are heavenly!

This book is a work of love. The Kitchen Witch is not just another cookbook. Oh yes, it features recipes you'll want to try, and once you do, will keep you coming back. But it's also part of a philosophy that will draw you in so that you too will be performing magic in your kitchen.

Bon appetite!

Chip Fraser – *Author of Philosophy of a Dashboard Saint*
www.dashboardsaint.us

Preface

Never trust a skinny cook. But, you can trust ME! It's all about the food, as long as I can remember. The best, the funnest, the feel good times in my life was all about the celebration with FOOD – tea parties with Grandma Ball, snacks in bed with Mom and TV when Dad was at the station, nightly dinners with Chip (the onion wars), Granddad's birthday party was more wonderful to me than Christmas! That's when Grandma Ball made clam chowder. Imagine growing up to look forward to May just for clam chowder, to see this little old white haired lady standing on a pink kitchen chair so she could stir the chowder in a huge pot (wish I had it!) – on top of a "little" gas stove! Deviled eggs were served too!

Another special food time for me was with my Aunt Vicki when she made custard. I loved it warm! She'd save a bite in the pan for me. Sweet, warm – I drank it like hot chocolate. It was good cold too. Tony's Hot Dogs, piquant cheese sandwiches at the old Smith and Welton Mezzanine – every Saturday! Then teenage years – not too hungry then, but it all came back when Chip and Pamela opened Potpourri Restaurant!

I think you know food or you don't! It's natural or forced. Everyone has family recipes they can do – but when you start cooking professionally, it's a whole new ball game! My recipes and style are rustique – solid. My cookbook will be easy to use and I hope we've covered some of your favorites of my signature dishes.

Remember, also, the five senses - SIGHT... SMELL... TOUCH... HEAR... TASTE! Feel free to work my recipes the way you want to! But not too much, because they are tried and true nightly with The Kitchen

Witch Catering.

A note about procedures - through years of experience, I have found it important to follow these procedures of my recipes for consistent results.

As an example, for the Fruit Crisp, use only 1 bowl. Do the fruit process/prep, then dump into baking dish and do flour, sugar mix in the same bowl. The flour crumb mixture will take on a pretty pale lilac color. So only wash the bowl once – when you are done!

I'm a lazy cook. The most bang for the least effort. Keep it simple stupid! The process makes the procedure easy to follow over and over again.

Oh – and always stay active or you'll become a fat cook too!

Observations

Through out the cookbook, for your enjoyment,

I have reflected on some of the passages

from my articles "The Bounty From the Banks"

that were published in the North Beach Sun

in the 1990's. They are not the full articles,

but are highlights of the Bounty of nature of

the Outer Banks of North Carolina.

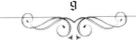

le Menu

Course One . . . Break The Fast

Course Two . . . Savories

Course Three . . . Snacks and Sides

le Menu

Course Four . . . Main Entrees

Atlantic Seafood Stew	65
N.C. Pulled Pork BBQ	67
Beef Wellington	69
Chicken Marsala	71
Summer Medley Bake ★	75
Medallions of Beef ★	77

Course Five . . . Sweet Stuff

Fruit Crisp	83
Cookie Dough Fruit Tart	85
Key Lime Pie	87
My Pecan Pie	91
Tropical Fruit Bread	93
Avalon Fruit Pie	95

By Mary Thrasher, Carova Beach, NC

"Secrets of the Sea
The Bounty of its Treasures
Keep coming to me!"

The story I am about to tell is true, and is one of the many reasons
why I want to help preserve the seclusion of our beaches from overuse!

ONE PORPOISE'S EPIPHANY!

It's been one weird weather summer, and July 25 was one of the wildest lightening storms I've ever been through! After a long day on the highway to Tidewater, my son Trey and I arrived in Corolla just as the front with its light show began. I stopped at Winks to let air out of the tires. Friends and neighbors were heading north home also. The fireworks of nature seem drawn to the open expanse of the Corolla beaches.

We followed a work truck loaded with ladders onto the strand and headed up. I've seen 20 years of wild weather on the Outer Banks, and I will never forget the color combination of the ocean, sky and lightening, turquoise sea and purple arcs of light against a slate grey sky.

I was scared and considered turning back when around a dune in the high tide tracks, we saw Pete and Margerite's blazer with their distress lights blinking. As we approached, Pete jumped out to flag me down. In the fray of the storm, their truck hit bottom, and they were stranded. Pete jumped in, and we drove back to A-1 Towing to notify Larry. Margerite stayed with the truck.

When we returned, the storm was more intense. We loaded their gear and took off north. The lightening cracked and the rain poured (like Carova needed more rain)! Once we went by the fire station to get mail, etc., the storm eventually cleared. Following good byes to friends, we slowly headed up to the beach home, a wet and, thankfully, empty beach.

I'll never know how or why (maybe the lightening knocked him out?) this innocent being came ashore, but I knew when I saw him, I had to do something. I

slammed on brakes and jumped out of the truck. The small, approximately 2-foot long bottle-nose dolphin cried and continued to struggle in the sand. He had dug his side flipper into the wet sand and was stuck in the out-going surf.

Without a thought, I attempted to grab his body. All muscle, the dolphin struggled, and I called for Trey to help. We picked him up again as I cradled him to my shoulder like a toddler and cooed "shh-shh". This creature was so perfect; pearl grey on top, pink on the underside. The body was soft as wet velvet and not a mark on it. Perfect!

I held on tight and waded into the surf up to my chest – dress, shoes and all. I let go, but he floated back. I caught him in my skirt and picked him up again. This time I waded out further, and held him over my head like a giant dart. I guess this presented a new perspective, because when I tossed him over the breakers, he knew just what to do. Off he went as he swam southeast without a glance back. We watched as he surfaced for air twice until we could not see any sign of him.

Thankfully, we were there when he needed help. It was the most wonderful experience of my life in Carova! Innocent, perfect, nature at its rawest! This innocent creature was alive, real and worth saving – regardless of any hassle.

That's exactly how I feel about Carova, too . . .

Course One
Break The Fast

Basic Custard for Quiche, Strata, Bread Pudding & French Toast

Suggestions & Process:

- Uses are endless for this custard.
- Custard fills one deep dish 9" pie shell. This custard is great for savory or sweet taste. Use it to fill your quiche, pie shells, pour over your strata/bread pudding casserole, or dip French bread for French toast.
- An excellent tenderizer for chicken and seafood.

Ingredients:

4 eggs
1 cup Half & Half
1/4 cup sour cream

Directions:

1. Whip ingredients until smooth. The more air incorporated into the custard base creates a more fluffy outcome.
2. Bake for quiche, strata, or bread pudding.
3. Refrigerate custard until use.

Take Note:

Quiche and other Egg Casseroles

Suggestion & Process:

- This custard is great for savory or sweet taste. Use it to fill your quiche or pour over your strata/bread pudding casserole.
- For quiche, use a pre baked 9" deep dish pie shell. Custard fills one deep dish 9" pie shell.
- For strata/bread pudding, use large, home made, 1" toasted bread cubes. Custard fills one 9 x 13" bake pan.

Ingredients:

- Assorted fillings suitable for both quiche & stratas:
- Shredded cheeses tossed with I Tbsp. Flour.
- Savory fillings such as cooked bacon, ham, sausage, assorted seafoods, left-overs are great, sauted onions, mushrooms, other vegetables.
- For bread pudding: pineapple, peaches, brown sugar, nuts.

Directions:

1. For quiche, in pre baked pie shell, assemble a bottom layer of 1/2 cup of desired fillings, at least one cup shredded cheese, and then pour custard over ingredients until pie shell is full.
2. Place assembled quiche on a sheet pan, bake in 350^0 oven for 50-60 minutes until set.
3. Let cool. For a meal portion, cut into quarters. For appetizer, cut into six pieces.

1. For strata/bread pudding, spray 9 x 13" baking pan with non stick spray. Place a single layer of bread cubes in baking pan.
2. Add 2 cups of desired fillings over bread cubes, 2 cups of shredded cheese, and pour enough custard to just cover casserole.
3. Assemble bread pudding in same manner.
4. Bake until set, approximately 20 to 40 minutes.

Take Note:

Slow down

As with times past, the horses, cows, and buffalo have been taking advantage of the cooler beach-front temperatures. Getting away from the flies.

The big fishing news this summer in one word: FLOUNDER! Many an evening tailgate party happened at the "ol'fishin'hole". Carova Lifestyles.

The old saying "Stop, and smell the roses" could be my theme song this year. My sunflowers are overhead. We've had a pasal of hummingbirds visit daily and my two hens have hatched two little chicks. We've had lots of company (and they better come back in the dead of winter too!). Fish fries on the beach, Crab & Blueberry feasts, and some of the most beautiful sky watching day or night that I can remember. All those late afternoon thunderstorms have created some spectacular sunsets! Good Friends. Good Food. Beautiful Entertainment. Mostly the Bounty from the Banks is good!

August 1994

Meals in a Muffin

Sweet and Savory

Suggestions & Process:

- This recipe includes items that are brand specific.
- There are two types of bases: a corn muffin base or a plain muffin base
- Optional fillings: bacon bits, cheese, cream cheese, jellies, veggies, seafood, herbs, and the list goes on . . .

Ingredients:

- Preferably use Jiffy corn muffin mix and Jiffy baking mix or comparable product in your grocery store.
- Eggs, oil, milk (according to muffin box directions)
- Paper baking cups (cupcake size)

Directions:

1. Prepare muffin mix according to directions on package
2. Assemble desired assorted fillings. Put paper baking cups in muffin tin and spray with non stick spray.
3. Put I Tbsp of muffin mix in the bottom of each paper baking cup.
4. Layer with 1 Tbsp of desired filling. Layer with additional muffin mix until paper baking cup is 2/3 full.
5. Bake according to directions on muffin box.
6. Note: muffins may be slightly moist due to the desired filling. Use "toothpick test" to check for doneness of muffins.

Take Note:

Frenchie French Toasts

Suggestions & Process:

- Can be served savory or sweet, can be stuffed, can be pre-prepped and pan grilled or baked.
- Toast can be stuffed or topped with assorted toppings: cheese, cream cheese, bacon bits, pineapple, nuts, use your imagination.

Ingredients:

- See base custard recipe.
- 1" diagonally sliced loaf bread (French or Italian bread)
- Assorted toppings
- Syrup, jams, powdered sugar, cinnamon

Directions:

1. For basic French Toast, dip pre sliced fresh bread into custard and grill in pan with butter or non stick pan spray until golden brown on each side.
2. For a stuffed French Toast, place desired assorted fillings between 2 slices of bread.
3. Dip in custard, grill in pan of butter or non stick pan spray.
4. Grill until golden brown on each side. Then finish in a 350^0 oven for 15 minutes. Serve hot with favorite topping.

Take Note:

Passion is a Strange Emotion

There is something magical about Harvest moons. This October has been a beautiful exception! Night shadows look velvet and move magically. While sleeping snug with Northeast breezes in my face, I'm awakened to footsteps outside my window. In the bright fullness, I see 4 of these velvet figures prancing in the wind driven moonlight! The few and proud wild horses of Carova.

It's been a big busy year! So many passages for people close to me. Such a crowded summer on the beach! I'm always so happy to see it slow down, cool off, and settle into the Holidays, family and friends time! Enjoy in health and happiness your special holiday season! The Bounty is there for our taking. Let's save and preserve it, FOREVER!

Fall 1995

Section 2
Savories

Hot Crab Dip

Suggestions & Process:

- Use a shallow baking dish sprayed with Pam spray to bake-off.
- Use a large sauté pan to combine ingredients
- Use ingredients that are room temperature.
- Serve with toast points and/or fancy crackers.
- Bake at 350° for 30 minutes/until bubbly.
- Use heavy wire whisk to combine ingredients and introduce air into the mixture.
- Precook ingredients and finish in the oven.

Ingredients:

1 stick of butter
1 bunch green onions (clean) just green tops
2 blocks (8 oz.) of cream cheese
1 Tbsp. of mayonnaise (Duke)
1 Tbsp. of sour crea
1 pound of jumbo blue crab meat.
Parmesan cheese for topping
Parsley (chopped)

Directions:

1. In a large sauté pan, melt butter with chopped green onion tops.
2. Add cream cheese, break up.
3. Whisk together until creamy and frothy, should be bubbling.
4. Using a spoon, add mayonnaise, sour cream, and crab meat. Combine gently.
5. Remove from heat and transfer to prepared baking pan.
6. Top with parmesan cheese and bake 350° for 20-30 minutes until bubbly.
7. 1 lb. of crabmeat serves approximately 10-20 people.

Take Note:

Baked Brie

Suggestions & Process:

- Serve with fancy crackers.
- Suggested additional toppings could be: sliced almonds and raspberry jam, pecans and brown sugar, pesto, sun dried tomatoes with garlic and parsley, chutney, salsa, sliced apples and peaches, etc.
- Brie will be enclosed in the puffed pastry and baked at 400° for approximately 20-30 minutes until Brie is melted and pastry is crispy brown.

Ingredients:

1 sheet of puffed pastry, partially thawed
Dusting of flour
8 ounce piece of Brie
Suggested additional toppings of your choice

Directions:

1. Dust work surface with flour.
2. Unfold pastry sheet onto surface.
3. Cut Brie into 2 pieces. Place both pieces onto pastry sheet, one piece on top of the other.
4. Place flavored topping on Brie.
5. Fold edges of pastry up into a purse like closure. Seal well.
6. Place in deep baking dish, at least 2 inches deep.
7. Bake in oven until crispy brown.
8. Serve and eat while hot.

Take Note:

Early Morning Autumn

Like daytime stars the migrating swallows swirled around us like snow in a snow dome. Against the blue of an early morning autumn sky, still showing a ¾ full harvest moon, I watched as they moved in waves and rhythms intoned to the ocean sounds in the distance. Minutes later they landed on a phone wire like pearls on a string! Oh Fall, my salvation and one of the many reasons I live in Carova! The "us" standing with me as I enjoyed the show, were 2 dogs and 3 black horses. I see them often on my walks, in addition to deer, foxes, rabbits and an occasional raccoon.

Fall 1996

Garlic Baked Shrimp

Suggestions & Process:

- This maybe served as an appetizer or a main course.
- Best when served hot, but maybe served at room temperature.
- Peel and devein shrimp. Tails may be left on or removed.
- Marinade shrimp for at least one hour.
- Place shrimp flat on a pre-sprayed baking sheet in a spoon to spoon design, for more uniform cooking.
- Bake at 350° for 15-20 minutes.
- Serve shrimp from pan with a spatula of 6-8 shrimp per serving.

Ingredients:

10-12 ounces bread crumbs (Plain or seasoned)
1 head of garlic (chopped)
1 cup of olive oil
3-5 lbs. of peeled and deveined medium to large shrimp

Directions:

1. Mix together bread crumbs, garlic, and olive oil.
2. Add shrimp and fold gently. Marinate in refrigerator for 1 hour.
3. Place on pan in single layer and bake until shrimp are pink and firm.

Take Note:

Sand Dollar Crab Cakes

Suggestions & Process:

- Only use blue crab.
- Use a savory mayonnaise for binding agent. (preferably Duke)
- Crush cornflakes with just your hands to smaller size, but still big and flaky.
- Make patties tight.
- Create 8 equal patties with the 1 pound of crab meat.
- Very important, refrigerate the patties at least 1 hour before baking.
- Bake at 350° for 20 - 30 minutes.

Ingredients:

1 pound of jumbo lump crabmeat
¼ cup of mayonnaise (plus, enough to bind)
1 small box (12 oz.) Cornflakes cereal
1 sticks of butter, cut into 1/2" pieces

Directions:

1. Combine crabmeat with mayonnaise. Fold gently, but thoroughly, incorporating ingredients and leaving crabmeat as whole as possible.
2. Divide mixture into 8 equal portions and make into 8 tight patties.
3. Spread one cup uncrushed cornflakes on baking sheet and reserve.
4. In shallow pan place 2 cups crushed cornflakes.
5. Liberally cover crabmeat portions/patties with crushed cornflakes.
6. Place on uncrushed cornflake baking sheet, top each crabcake with 1/2 tsp. butter and refrigerate.
7. Bake patties until golden brown.
8. Carefully remove patties and place on a fresh uncrushed cornflake platter.
9. Eat immediately or place in a low temperature (250⁰) oven.

Take Note:

A Different Walk

It's a different walk I take on a winter's beach. The spring brings a hint of the Gulf stream, the summer the need for a hat, the fall beach is ever changing. But the winter beach is still, and quiet. The air is cold and certain. The tire tracks are fewer. The birds huddle together. There are still treasures to be found, but not everyday, for all it takes is a Nor'easter to move in and like an autumn storm, everything is washed away or sand covered by the wind! And should a snow accompany the blow and all vistas but the ocean become the same!

Breaking down or getting stuck on the beach has a totally different meaning in the winter! A long cold wait for help could be unpleasant without provisions! Brandy in a cask around any dog's neck is a welcoming sight, after an hour or so! Especially on a foggy night! Happy New Year! The term "from the kindness of stangers" is so true. And friends who help you out are the best to be found.

Finally, spring brings so much bounty — more people, parties, more traffic, more noise; it also brings more wildlife. We have one new baby colt so far — we haven't seen it yet, but we have seen its tracks and they're the size of fifty cent piece! Precious!

Mary! Quite contrary! The work required for this lifestyle sometimes cancels out WHY I live here. But then I hear the snow geese fly overhead, I see a footprint in the snow covered sand and can hear and smell the ocean from my front porch; and something makes me want to continue to discover the Bounty from the Banks, and to help preserve it.

February 1996

French Herbal Cheese Spread

Suggestions & Process:

- May roll into a large ball or a log roll.
- May roll into smaller portion sized rolls.
- Refrigeration necessary.
- Serve chilled.
- An excellent sauce when baked on chicken

Ingredients:

4 - 8 ounce blocks of cream cheese (softened)
1 stick of butter (softened)
1 head of garlic (finely chopped)
1 tsp. Salt
1 cup mixed fresh herbs (chopped)
    Rosemary
    Thyme
    Oregano
    Chives
1 Tbsp. Dried parsley
1 Tbsp. Parmesan cheese

Directions:

- Mix all ingredients well and refrigerate
- Form into ball or log, or... use your imagination!.

Take Note:

Course 3
Snacks & Sides

Monte Cristo Veggie Sandwich

Suggestions & Process:

Slice veggies thin, veggies can be cooked if preferred.
Use fresh rye or a hearty wheat bread.
Sandwich is dipped in an egg wash and then grilled like French toast.
This makes one sandwich.

Ingredients:

1 Egg
2 oz. milk
2 slices of bread
1 tablespoon butter
1 tablespoon of ranch dressing or Thousand Island salad dressing
1 leaf of lettuce
6 thin slices of cucumber
Half of green/red pepper (sliced thin)
2 slices thin, red onion
2 ounces alfalfa sprouts
2 slices of white cheese (muenster, provolone, or swiss)

Directions:

Melt butter on pan surface or a flat grill on low to medium heat.
Dip one side of sliced breads in egg and milk mixture.
Place bread slices on top of melted butter of pan.
Put equal amounts of dressing on both slices of bread.
Put equal amounts of cheese on both slices of bread.
Stack the veggies on one slice of bread.
Fold cheese slice bread onto veggie slice bread and slightly compress.
Cook this side for 5 minutes then flip to other side for 5 more minutes.

Take Note:

Savory Chicken Salad
with Garlic Pickles

Suggestions & Process:

- Use boneless, skinless chicken breast.
- Requires refrigeration.
- Lightly boil or bake chicken until done. Cut chicken into bite size pieces or tear or shred same size as cut ingredients.

Ingredients:

10-12 Boneless chicken breasts, dice/tear into 1" pieces
½ cup Savory mayonnaise (preferably Dukes mayonnaise)
Dollop sour cream
2 celery stalks include celery leaves (cut into same size as diced chicken)
4 spears of Clausen garlic pickles
¾ cup pecan halves
¾ cup green onion tops
Salt and pepper

Directions:

1. Boil or bake chicken breast. Cool. Cut.
2. In a bowl, prepare mayonnaise, sour cream, and salt and pepper.
3. Add remaining ingredients, including chicken, to dressing, stir well. Refrigerate.
4. Serve as salad or sandwich

Take Note:

Extreme Caesar Salad Dressing

Suggestions & Process:

- This recipe is for a large salad to feed 10 people.
- Recommend using Romaine lettuce or lettuce greens.
- Follow ingredients as listed, the parmesan cheese helps to emulsify garlic and anchovies.
- This is an eggless Caesar dressing and does not need to be chilled before service.

Ingredients:

10 gloves of garlic (peeled)
2 ounce can of anchovies
1 tablespoon parmesan cheese
1 tablespoon Dijon mustard
1/8 cup of balsamic vinegar
1 cup of olive oil (good quality)

Directions:

1. Using a small food processor, process garlic until finely chopped.
2. Add anchovies and then parmesan cheese. Process after addition.
3. Add Dijon mustard. Process after addition.
4. Add balsamic vinegar and process until mixture is smooth.
5. Add olive oil and process until smooth.

Serve with lettuce and homemade croutons.
Optional ingredients: assorted salad vegetables, grilled chicken, grilled steak.

Take Note:

Winter's Observation

Winter's Desolation,

Winter's Consolation,

Empty Beaches,

Seagull Speeches,

Seafoam flying,

Conch shells Arriving,

Changeless yet,

Like the Tide

Changing much too fast!

Party Mash Potatoes

Suggestions & Process:

- Use little red potatoes
- Cut potatoes, wash cubes and drain
- Use a hand held potato masher.
- Bake at 350° or until golden around edges.

Ingredients:

5 pounds potatoes
1 head garlic (minced)
Water (to boil)
1-8 ounce block cream cheese
2 sticks butter
1 quart half and half
1-8 ounce container sour cream
Salt and pepper (to taste)
Parmesan cheese

Directions:

1. Cube potatoes into 1½ " chunks (skins on).
2. Clean garlic.
3. Place potatoes and garlic together, boil until fork slides easily through potato.
4. Drain.
5. In the same pot put butter, cream cheese, half and half, and sour cream.
6. Put potatoes and garlic back into pot and mash together to desired smoothness. Chunks in potatoes are good chews.
7. Salt and pepper to taste.
8. Put in baking dish and top with butter and parmesan cheese.
9. Bake at 350° or until golden around edges.

Take Note:

Corny Cornbread

Suggestions & Process:

- Serve warm with butter and honey.
- Excellent for breakfast toasted in the oven.
- Bake at 350° - 400° until golden brown.

Ingredients:

4 boxes of Jiffy brand corn bread mix
2 cans of cream corn
4 eggs
½ cup of oil
1 cup of half and half
1 tablespoon brown sugar

Directions:

1. Mix wet ingredients in a bowl with sugar.
2. Add corn bread mix. Do not over stir.
3. Spray 2 9x13 baking pans.
4. Bake approximately 20 - 30 minutes until golden brown.

Take Note:

Wild Wind Riders

By Blanche B. Miller 1990

EDITOR'S NOTE: Written back in 1990 about typical day living among the wild ones of the North Beaches, the following passages tell of a time since long passed when places, people and things were still beheld in awe and yet to be fully understood. Our surroundings here and everything that comes with it were perhaps simpler, slower and less taken for granted. Much open land still existed, traffic jams were not the norm and the quiet beaches of Carova, and yes, Corolla were yet to be maxed out with mansions, motors and mobs. In their words, it was a land where wild horses still roamed. In just five, almost six, short years, so much ahs changed — the streets are not safe for such roaming; the beaches no longer tranquil. A select few have sacrificed plenty to assure of their safety, yet these horses are still not safe, protected or truly free . . . to SURVIVE. What's it gonna take? Answers re unknown, fate is unclear, but we are occupants of these beaches can take the time to remember, to reflect back on what it was that brought us here in the first palce. Maybe it wasn't necessarily the horses, but I'm pretty sure it had to do with something more, something WILD . . .

Try to imagine waking up at the break of dawn at the seashore. You recall the sound of the breaking waves lulling you to sleep last night. Now you hear a new sound and can't believe your ears. Horses are snorting and whinnying and neighing. The sounds are coming from beneath the house. Then you remember that the house is built on stilts. You're on the northern Outer Banks of North Carolina.

You are awakened by a family of wild horses: a stallion, a mare, and a colt. There are approximately fifty wild horses that roam in an area of twenty miles by one mile wide. They are descendants of the Spanish mustangs and have been part of this barrier reef environment since 1543. That's when the Spanish expeditions brought them here. The Spanish colonization was successful and the horses were left behind.

These horses are the only true Spanish mustang heard in the world still living in the wild. Old-timers in this areas delight in repeating stories they've heard down through the years about how the Cherokees, Chickasaws and the Choctaws took many of the horses on their forced migration west. The Indians named their 1,200 mile trek "Trail of Tears". It's reported that the Indians safe arrival; and continued survival were entirely due to these horses.

Today, these wild and free horses are a surprising delight to visitors to this area. To residents they are precious and well protected. A wild horse sanctuary has been established to prohibit the killing, trapping, injuring, tormenting or taking of wild horses. If there is an accident that injures a horse, it is a violation not to report it immediately. Civilization has indeed caught up with these mustangs. They seldom leave the developed

area to forage in the wilderness because they prefer the cultivated grass. The Wild Horse Sanctuary issues "Save Our Wild Horses" T-shirts and bumper stickers proclaiming "I Brake for Wild Horses."

Signs have been set up along traffic areas warning "Wild Horse Crossings" and "Horses on Road at Night."

William Shakespeare wrote of the Wild Horse:

> "Sometimes he scuds far off, and there he stares;
> Anon he starts at stirring of a feather:
> To bid the wind a bases he now prepares,
> And we'r he run or fly they know no whether;
> For through his mane and tail the high wind sings,
> Fanning the hairs, who wave like feathered wings."

You may be snuggled in bed one night in a house that resembles a giant spider. You hear the wild wind screaming off the ocean. Now listen carefully for the sudden drumming of hooves riding the same wild wind. In the morning you awaken and call out to the mustangs you've named Midnight, Molly and Star.

A resident of Kill Devil Hills since 1981, Blanche Miller loves to read and write about local history.

Artist Troy THRASHER 1998

Course 4
Main Entrees

Gifts from the Sea

Sometimes we take for granted our bountiful gifts from the sea; we forget how delicate life and our planet is. One cloudy, off shore day, my friends Becky, Trey and I found a seahorse. The water was frigid and we found him on the low tide. It was barely alive and damaged. We find all sorts of treasures on our walks, summer and winter alike, but I have never found a seahorse washed ashore. I knew it was hurt and probably wouldn't live, but it wrapped its tail around my finger as if to say "I'm Alive" – there is hope! I waded out to quiet waters and released my gift from the sea. It's not likely I'll ever find another, very rare on shore; but releasing it gave me some Hope; for a time of Awareness!

Atlantic Seafood Stew

Suggestions & Process:

- Hearty bowlful perfect with crusty bread.
- Similar to a bouillabaise.
- Serve with garlic mayonnaise and crusty bread.
- Recommended serving portion is, (example) 6 clams, 4 scallops, 8 shrimp per person.
- All vegetables and seafood should be cut at the same size. Use freshest, seasonal ingredients available.
- This recipe serves 4 people.

Ingredients:

2 medium size onions, 1" pieces
1 head celery stem and leaves, 1" pieces
4 cloves garlic, minced
Olive oil or butter
Fresh herbs, such as thyme, parsley
24 shrimp, peeled, leave tail on
16 large sea scallops, cut in half
1 pound of firm, white fish (example Rockfish, Cod, or Halibut), cut into 2" pieces
16 ounce can of broth, fish or chicken
24 cherry or little neck clams, in shell
24 mussels, de bearded in shell
16 ounce can of diced tomato
Fresh parsley
Optional seafood: crab, lobster tail, calamari

Directions:

1. Sauté vegetables, garlic, and herbs in butter or olive oil.
2. Add shrimp, scallops, and fish. Stir gently and simmer.
3. Add broth and shell fish.

(Next page)

4. Simmer half hour low heat.
5. Add chopped tomato and fresh parsley.
6. Serve with garlic mayonnaise.

Take Note:

North Carolina Pulled Pork BBQ

Suggestions & Process:

- Three pork butts will feed 10-20 people nicely. Shred pork after baking while in the pan.
- Baked, boiled and shredded.
- This recipe needs to be prepared in two days. Cook the pork butts a day in advance and then prepare the barbeque the following day. Use three fresh pork butts or shoulders, baked and roasted the day before in the oven for 350° for 20-30 minutes per pound until outside of pork is crusty brown. Cool in the refrigerator over night. The next day before simmering, remove layer of white fat from the pork and reserve the pork jelly.

Ingredients:

3 fresh pork butts or shoulders
   (approximately 6 pounds each)
2 cups of water
1 cup sugar
¼ cup red pepper flakes (adjust to taste)
1 cup white or apple cider vinegar
1 bottle of vinegar based barbeque sauce
   (suggest Scott's brand)
Coleslaw (as preferred)

Directions:

1. In a large stock pot, place the pork butts and pork jelly, and add two cups of water, cup of sugar, and ¼ cup of red pepper flakes.
2. Begin boiling and add 1 cup of vinegar. Stir often to prevent sticking. Boil moderately for at least three hours, covered.
3. Shred meat and remove the bones as the meat separates.

Take Note:

Beef Wellington

Suggestions:

- If you do not know how to clean the tenderloin, have your butcher clean and strip the tenderloin.
- Cut tenderloin in half for 2 roasts (chateaubriand).
- You can use an egg wash brushed on pastry before baking.
- Thaw pastry.
- Bake in pastry at 400° or until pastry is brown and crispy
- Use a little flour on board when working with the dough.
- Do not pre-cook beef.

Ingredients:

Full Beef Tenderloin, stripped, peeled, cut in half
Butter
2 packs mushroom (chopped)
2 sheets Puff Pastry
1 lb. Virginia salt ham (sliced paper thin)

Directions:

1. Clean tenderloin of Beef.
2. Sauté chopped mushrooms in pat of butter. Cook until dry.
3. Lay out puff pastry, then lay thinly sliced ham, and spread with mushroom mix.
4. Place Beef on pastry and mushroom/ham mix and roll to cover beef. Close ends as well as possible. Place on pan seam side down.
5. Bake at 400-450 degrees until pastry is crisp brown.
6. Make bleu cheese sauce for topping after Wellington is sliced in 1½ - 2" slices.

(Next page)

Bleu Cheese Sauce:

Butter
Flour (to thicken)
Half and half or heavy cream
1-4 ounce cube Bleu cheese

1. Melt butter and add flour with a whisk.
2. Mix well together and start adding half and half to get a medium thick sauce.
3. Crumble bleu cheese and stir until cheese melts and sauce is smooth with a pale grey, blue color.
4. Serve with steamed veggies and Beef Wellington baked potatoes.

Take Note:

Chicken Marsala

Suggestions & Process:

- This recipe is at its best when prepared with a good quality Marsala wine.
- Stove top preparations should be a quick fix. The recipe will be finished and cooked in the oven.
- Bake at 350° after pan preparations for 30-40 minutes until sauce is bubbly.

Ingredients:

10-12 Boneless chicken breasts, cut into 3" strips
Flour
1 cup olive oil (divided)
1 stick butter (divided)
1 quart ½ and ½ or heavy cream
1 quart (plus) Marsala Wine
4 packages of 8 ounce mushrooms (sliced)

Directions:

1. Dust chicken strips with flour and brown in ½ cup of the olive oil and half stick of the butter until crispy. Add additional olive oil and butter as necessary to brown chicken. Place brown chicken strips side by side in baking/roasting pan.
2. In fry pan with reserved oil and crispy bits, add flour to brown and some ½ and ½ to loosen crispy bits. Use a wire whisk. Keep building sauce with ½ and ½ and Marsala wine until there is enough sauce to cover chicken.
3. Add sliced mushrooms to sauce.
4. Immediately pour mixture over browned chicken strips.
5. Bake in 350° oven until done approximately 30-40 minutes.
6. Can cover, but remove cover to finish up.

Take Note:

New Life

We saw our first osprey of the spring, swooping and searching over the shallows looking for his vittles! That isn't the only activity on the beaches! The mild winter weekend's weather hints of the new life approaching.

Our wild horses look so beautiful in their winter velvet coats. The winter has been kind to most, although they've had few acorns to eat. The will get their fill of sea oats in August.

We all love this place, we'll have our memories. We'll make some more! But like sand sifting through your fingers, the way it was - is gone forever!

February 1997

Summer Medley Bake

Suggestions & Process:

- Best served with rice or couscous. Use fresh ingredients for best results.
- Peel and devein shrimp with tails off. Cut fish into bite size pieces. Recommend a light and flaky fish such as flounder or halibut. Choose young tender summer vegetables such as yellow squash, scallion onions, and young tender celery. Tomatoes may be added.
- Combine all ingredients to obtain a broth.
- Bake at 350° for 20 - 30 minutes until bubbly and shrimp are pink.
- Makes a wonderful broth.

Ingredients:

1 pound of sea scallops
1 pound of jumbo lump crab meat
1 pound of peeled shrimp
1 pound of mild, flaky white fish
2 small summer yellow squash
1 bunch scallion onions, cut
1 stick of butter
Juice of 4 lemons
Salt and pepper to taste

Directions:

Cut all ingredients into bite size pieces.
Combine all ingredients and place into a pre-sprayed baking dish.
Cut butter into 8 equal pieces and distribute evenly over contents.
Pour lemon juice evenly over contents.
Salt and pepper to taste.
Bake until shrimp are pink and broth is bubbly.
Recommend using the broth as a sauce.

Take Note:

Medallions of Beef Tenderloin

Suggestions & Process:

- If you do not know how to clean the tenderloin, have your butcher clean and strip the tenderloin.
- Cut tenderloin in half so that you have 2 roasts (chateaubriand)
- Bake the 2 roasts at 350° for 20 minutes. They will appear very rare and juicy. Let cool and slice into ½ inch medallions.
- Lay medallions like shingles on a cookie sheet or flat roasting pan.
- Bake additional 20 minutes or until desired doneness before service.
- Best rare to medium rare... so tender!

Ingredients:

Full Beef Tenderloin, stripped and peeled, cut in half
1 tablespoon Horseradish
1 cup Mayonnaise
1 tablespoon Sour cream

Directions:

1. Follow process above in preparing beef medallions.
2. Mix horseradish, mayonnaise, and sour cream for sauce.

Take Note:

Course 5
Sweet Stuff

Rural Joy

There is a natural phenomenon that occurs in rural America. Noisy night sounds begin at dusk, continuing into the wee morning hours! Without city sounds, you can actually hear the crickets, frogs and the whip-o-will call. Sometime with the addition of the oceans roar, it's so loud you can't get to sleep!

A rainy and cool April has encouraged lonely beaches and green trails. Carova Beaches are happy to welcome at least 2 new ponies. We've named one red female colt "Comet" because of a comma shaped star on her forehead! She's so excited to be here! Jumping and galloping all over the place! Her stallion ancestor and his new bride come to my house everyday to eat grass. He is red with a comma shaped mark on his forehead and so I've named him Comma.

May 1997

Fruit Crisp

Suggestions & Process:

- Serve hot/warm over vanilla ice cream.
- Baked at 350° until bubbly and crust is golden brown.

Ingredients:

2 sticks butter
2 cups sugar
1 cup flour
2 fresh apples (skin on/cut into small bite size pieces)
1 pear (skin on/cut into small bite size pieces)
2 cups of sugar plus ½ cup of sugar
2 12 oz. bag frozen mixed fruit (strawberry, blackberry, blueberry)
1 12 oz. bag frozen peaches

Directions:

1. Melt butter - do not burn. (Can be done in a microwave)
2. Add melted butter to 2 cups of sugar and flour until crumbly.
3. Combine all fruit (fresh and frozen) add ½ cup sugar and mix well.
4. Pour into deep, greased baking dish.
5. Cover top with crumb mix.
6. Bake until brown and bubbly, about 45 minutes.

Take Note:

Cookie Dough Fruit Tart

Suggestions & Process:

- Use store bought rolled sugar cookie dough. One large roll will fill one 13 x 9 cookie sheet.
- This is an oven to refrigerator dessert.

Ingredients:

1 rolled sugar cookie dough
1 pint fresh strawberries (cleaned and sliced)
1 pint fresh blueberries
3 kiwis (peeled, sliced ¼" thick, and sliced in half)
2 cans sweetened condensed milk
1 cup lemon, lime, or orange juice
2 eggs
1 jar of apple jelly

Directions:

1. Spread sugar cookie dough out on sprayed cookie sheet, forming an edge.
2. Poke cookie dough with a fork.
3. Bake cookie dough in oven 2/3 of suggested cooking time from the cookie package directions.
4. Remove and cool cooked cookie dough.
5. While the cookie dough is cooling, prepare custard by mixing the 2 cans of sweetened condensed milk with the 2 eggs. Incorporate well and then add the citrus juice. Mix mixture well with whisk.
6. Pour and spread custard on the cooled cookie dough.
7. Bake the additional 1/3 cooking time from the cookie package directions.
8. Remove and cool.
9. Place a line of sliced strawberries across the prepared custard.

(Next page)

10. Slightly warm apple jelly with small amount of water just until mixture can consistently glaze the fruit on top.
11. Refrigerate and enjoy.

Take Note:

Key Lime Pie

Suggestions & Process:

- Incorporate eggs with milk before adding the lime juice. This will make 1 large (extra serving) pie or 2 small (regular serving) pies.
- This is an oven to refrigerator dessert.

Ingredients:

2 cans of sweetened condensed milk
1 8 ounce jar of Real Lime juice
2 eggs
1 large (extra serving) graham cracker crust or 2 (regular serving) graham cracker crust
Garnish with sliced lime

Directions:

1. Combine sweetened condensed milk with eggs. Incorporate well.
2. Add lime juice. Whisk well until fluffy.
3. Pour into prepared graham cracker crust.
4. Bake in oven at 350o for 12-15 minutes. Do not allow the custard to brown.
5. Remove and refrigerate until completely cooled.
6. Upon serving, garnish with sliced lime.

Take Note:

Carova Rovers

There is a special time of day when certain atmosphere conditions prevail, a half grayness, slick glassy water, mist from the marsh, right before sun up when the sky and the ocean horizons meld into one another and become one continuous ethereal void, no beginning no ending. I've witnessed this natural phenomenon many times in all seasons.

Magically, the beaches have cleared out (except weekends) and cleaned up, thanks partly to the few Nor'east blows we've had. Fishing has been terrific this fall. Our coffers are full! We'll be eating fish fried, caked, baked, broiled, corned and salted for many months to come!

Bounty can be delicious! Just go out and get it!
Da Bounty Be Good to Me!

Fall 1994

My Pecan Pie

Suggestions:

- Serve with ice cream or whipped cream.
- Can add 1/3 cup cocoa or chocolate chips to this if you prefer chocolate pecan pie.
- Bake in oven at 350°.

Ingredients:

2 9 inch deep dish frozen pie shells
2 cups brown sugar
8 eggs
3 cups pecan halves (divided)
2 sticks of butter (melted)
1 tsp. vanilla

Directions:

1. Add sugar to melted butter. Combine. Add vanilla.
2. Add 2 cups of the pecans. Combine.
3. Pour into pie shells equally.
4. Divide remaining 1 cup of pecans in half to sprinkle evenly on the top of the 2 pies.
5. Bake in oven at 350o for 30-40 minutes until set.
6. Remove from oven. Maybe served warm or cooled as preferred.

Take Note:

Tropical Fruit Bread

Suggestions:

This is a sugar free recipe, but sugar can be added. I would suggest 1 cup brown sugar, honey or molasses. Also try 1/2 cup Splenda brown sugar. Sugar or Splenda would be added to dry ingredients, honey or molasses to the wet ingredients.
Bake at 350° for one hour or until golden brown.

Ingredients:

Dry ingredients:
2 cups Bran flakes
2 cups self rising flour
2 cups whole wheat flour
2 cups oatmeal
Fruits and Nuts:
1 1/2 cups whole walnuts
1/2 cup pecans
1 cup cranraisins
2 cups coconut
1 cup chopped prunes
1 15 oz. can pineapple chunks (reserve juice)

Wet ingredients:
4 eggs
1 cup milk
1/2 cup orange juice plus reserved pineapple juice
1 tbsp vanilla
1 cup oil

Directions:

(Next page)

1. Use 3 large mixing bowls: one bowl for dry ingredients, one bowl for filling, one bowl for wet ingredients.
2. Combine well mixed dry ingredients with fruit and nuts.
3. Mix wet ingredients with a whisk.
4. Incorporate wet ingredients slowly with large spoon to the dry mixture. If too dry, add additional milk or juice.
5. Pour mixture equally into 3 bread loaf pans generously sprayed with non stick pan spray.
6. Bake at 350⁰ for at least one hour or to the clean "toothpick test".
7. Serve warm from oven or can be reheated sliced in toaster oven or oven.

Take Note:

Avalon Fruit Pie

Suggestions & Process:

- Serve with ice cream or whipped cream.
- Bake at 350^0 for one hour or until golden brown.

Ingredients:

2 9" pre baked deep dish pie shells
4 eggs
1 stick butter
1 cup brown sugar
1 cup pecans
1 cup raisins or cranraisins
1 cup coconut
1 15 oz. can pineapple chunks (drained)

Directions:

1. Combine wet ingredients with a whisk or mixer until well incorporated.
2. Combine well mixed dry ingredients with wet ingredients.
3. Pour mixture equally into 2 pre baked pie shells.
4. Bake at 350^0 for 50-60 minutes until golden brown.

Take Note:

Pantry List

Specific brands I use:

- Duke's Mayonaise
- Jiffy Cornbread Mix
- Jiffy or Bisquick Biscuit Mix
- Self-rising Flour
- Bread & Butter Pickles
- Scott's BBQ Sauce
- Grey Poupon Dijon Mustard
- Heinz Ketchup
- Paul Newman Balsamic Vinegarette
- Bush's Baked Beans
- Champion Horse Radish
- Clausen Garlic Pickles
- Kraft Ready Parmesan
- Breyers Ice Cream
- Hidden Valley Ranch
- Real Lime Juice
- Borden Sweetened Condensed Milk

Visit www.TheKitchenWitchCatering.com
and check out the original
Kitchen Witch Catering items available in the Gift Shop!

• T-shirts • Hats • Aprons • Tote Bags
are just a few of our products

*Franchise Information will be available
Fall of 2008!*

The Kitchen Witch Catering Company was founded by Mary M. Thrasher, a long time resident of the Outer Banks. Through the years she has worked at many of the finer restaurants on the Outer Banks, as well as in Norfolk, Virginia. She is well-traveled and attended the New York Restaurant School. Mary has developed and designed menus for 20 years and can help you design your perfect menu and party. Whether for 2 or 200 each party, reception or dinner is treated with the same attention to detail and personal attention

For more information, contact:

Mary M. Thrasher
Phone: (252) 453-2260
E-mail: mkitchenwitch@aol.com

Bewitch friends and family this year and treat yourself to a once-in-a-lifetime luxury vacation by having "The Kitchen Witch" brew up some culinary magic in your home.

- Anniversaries
- Holidays
- Cocktail Parties
- Tea Parties
- Dessert Parties
- Special Packages

- Birthdays
- Luncheons
- Menus Available
- Cooking Lessons
- Shopping
- Family Reunions

- Intimate Gatherings (2-200)
- Brunches
- Christmas Baking
- Seafood Specialties
- Dinner Parties
- Staff Available

From Artichokes to Ziti... we do it all!